What Right to Strike?

ARTHUR SHENFIELD

with Commentaries by

CYRIL GRUNFELD

SIR LEONARD NEAL

Published by

THE INSTITUTE OF ECONOMIC AFFAIRS

1986

First published in April 1986

by

THE INSTITUTE OF ECONOMIC AFFAIRS

2 Lord North Street, Westminster, London SW1P 3LB

© The Institute of Economic Affairs 1986

ISSN 0073-2818

ISBN 0-255 36190-4

Printed in Great Britain by

GORON PRO-PRINT CO LTD, LANCING, WEST SUSSEX

Set in Monotype Plantin 11 on 12 point

CONTENTS

PREFACE

The *Hobart Papers* are intended to contribute a stream of authoritative, independent and lucid analysis to the understanding and application of economics to private and government activity. The characteristic theme has been the optimum use of scarce resources and the extent to which it can best be achieved in markets within an appropriate framework of laws and institutions or, where markets cannot work, in other ways. Since in the real world the alternative to the market is the state, and both are imperfect, the choice between them effectively turns on a judgement of the comparative consequences of 'market failure' and 'governmental failure'.

The appropriate framework of laws and institutions within which the labour market should operate has been a matter of controversy at least since the early years of this century. Trade union spokesmen often claim that the law has no place at all in union activity. But opinion has increasingly come to the view that the role of trade unions should be much more closely defined in law and the major legislation introduced in 1980, 1982 and 1984 has become more widely accepted.

From its beginning the IEA has given a strong lead to this debate. One of its earliest titles, in 1959, was *Trade Unions in a Free Society* by B. C. (now Professor) Roberts, which both reminded British trade unions of the very different role played by unions in America and advised them 'to come to terms with the market economy'. A few years later, in *Unions and Prosperity* (Hobart Paper 6), Frank Bealey and Stephen Parkinson noted the decline in public sympathy for unions and offered proposals to make them more compatible with growing affluence.

Against the background of a general rise in standards of living and fall in support for union behaviour, a re-appraisal of their role and legal standing became inevitable. In 1973 Charles Hanson issued the challenge of *Trade Unions: A Century of Privilege?* (Occasional Paper 38), followed by the proceedings of a seminar

[5]

in 1977, published with a no less provocative title – *Trade Unions: Public Goods or Public 'Bads'?* (IEA Readings 17).

IEA authors have also devoted attention to many other aspects of the labour market in *The Restrictive Society* by John Lincoln, (1967), *Can Workers Manage?* (Hobart Paper 77) on co-determination, and *1980s Unemployment and the Unions* (Hobart Paper 87), in which Professor F. A. Hayek analyses the role of trade unions in the causation of inflation and unemployment.

Despite changes in law and other policies, the labour market is still far from working properly, as is shown by the substantial increase in unemployment in the 1980s, accompanied by a rise, not a fall, in wage costs. One explanation may be the continuation of what Professor Hutt has called the 'strike-threat system'. That this has been tolerated for so long, in spite of its disastrous effect on output and real wages, testifies to the stubborn hold on the public mind of the argument that labour is everywhere and always at a disadvantage in 'bargaining' with capital. A decade ago, the Institute reprinted an extended edition of Professor Hutt's pioneering work, *The Theory of Collective Bargaining*, originally published in 1930, in which this 'disadvantage' is critically examined, and judged unconvincing.

In this latest *Hobart Paper*, Arthur Shenfield concentrates on the single, fundamental issue of the right to strike. He makes it clear that the only right which can be made compatible with a free society is quite different from the kind of strike with which we have been familiar in recent years. The strike weapon may be justified as any man's right to withdraw his labour. But in most strikes the workers do not so much withdraw their labour, as no longer perform their jobs whilst insisting that their labour remains available for 'their' jobs. In effect, they claim that the jobs belong to them.

The author also examines the confusion surrounding the unique legal status of unions, which are not bodies corporate, but have some of the rights and powers which bodies corporate enjoy. Mr Shenfield puts forward 14 proposals for reform of trade unions, which would transform them into institutions giving their members the positive services they need to prosper in a free labour market.

To help readers understand these proposals and the arguments that lead to them, commentaries on the *Paper* were invited from

[6]

two leading figures in the world of labour relations, one an academic, the other a practitioner. Professor Cyril Grunfeld was Professor of Law at the London School of Economics from 1966 to 1982 and has written widely on many aspects of industrial relations. Sir Leonard Neal was Labour Relations Adviser to Esso Petroleum at the time of the Fawley experiment, and was Chairman of the Commission on Industrial Relations from 1971 to 1974.

Although the Institute's constitution requires that its Directors, Trustees and Advisers are formally dissociated from the author's conclusions, this *Paper* is offered as a stimulating and original contribution, by an experienced and thoughtful barrister and economist, towards wider public understanding of what is still one of Britain's most intractable problems.

March 1986   JOHN B. WOOD

THE AUTHOR

ARTHUR A. SHENFIELD is a former Economic Director of the Federation of British Industries (1955-64) and the Confederation of British Industry (1964-67). From 1967-69 he was Director of the Industrial Policy Group. He had previously been Assistant Editor of the London and Cambridge Economic Service and Lecturer in Economics at the University of Birmingham. A Lord Justice Holker Exhibitioner of Gray's Inn, he practised at the Bar from 1945-55.

In recent years he has been a Visiting Professor at various American universities: Professor of Economics of Industry at the University of Chicago Graduate School of Business (twice); Regents' Professor of Economics at the University of California; Professor of Law of Competition and Monopoly at the University of San Diego Law School; Professor of Economics at the University of Dallas; Distinguished Professor of Mineral Economics at the Colorado School of Mines; Distinguished Professor of Economics at Rockford College, Illinois; Ludwig von Mises Distinguished Professor of Economics at Hillsdale College, Michigan.

In 1972-74 he was President of the Mont Pélèrin Society. From 1959 to 1984 he was External Examiner in the Economics of Industry at the University of London.

GLOSSARY

A.E.R. – All England Law Reports.

A.C. – Appeal Cases (House of Lords).

Q.B. – Queen's Bench Reports.

PART I

WHAT IS A STRIKE?

Definitions

WHAT IS a strike? In Tramp Shipping *v.* Greenwich Marine Inc.,[1] Lord Denning, Master of the Rolls, defined it as

> 'a concerted stoppage of work by men done with a view to improving their wages or conditions, or giving vent to a grievance, or making a protest about something or other, or supporting or sympathising with other workmen, in such endeavours'.

In Para. 24(1), Schedule 13 of the Employment Protection (Consolidation) Act, 1978, a strike was defined as

> 'the cessation of work by a body of persons employed acting in combination, or a concerted refusal, or a refusal under a common understanding, of any number of persons employed in consequence of a dispute, done as a means of compelling their employer or any person or body of persons employed, or to aid other employees in compelling their employer, to accept or not to accept terms or conditions of or affecting employment'.

But these definitions give us little guidance. We all know that when workers strike they down tools or walk out because of some alleged grievance or disagreement about their or other workers' wages or conditions of work. But this gives only a limited insight into the strikers' motivations. It tends to confirm the generally prevailing view that a strike is a manifestation of conflict between workers and employers. It diverts attention from the possibility that the true conflict may be between worker and worker (and not just a worker who, as in the second definition above, is employed by the same employer, but one who is outside that employment). Thus in a highly esteemed economics textbook a strike is defined as '. . . an attempt to prevent other sellers of labour from offering

---

[1] 1975 2AER 989.

[9]

their services at rates (or working conditions) lower than those sought by the striking employees'.[1] In another important book, this aspect of strikes is clarified thus:

> 'Nor are strikes the much-ballyhooed conflict between management and labour (a form of buyer-seller conflict), because labour, capital, and management services basically are co-operating factors in the management process. Instead, strikes expose the basic conflict among competing sellers in the market for labour services, namely the conflict between organised labour and unorganised labour. Stated in the earthy (and divisive) idiom of unionism, the central problem for unions is the existence of "scabs", "rats", and "strikebreakers", not the presence of capitalists, investors vexed by excessive greed, or large corporations. A successful strike depends on the union's ability to persuade *everyone* to strike.'[2]

Rights and remedies

Since our subject is the right to strike, we must first consider the view of this right habitually presented by apologists for strikers as so obviously true as hardly needing to be stated, even though it is controverted by the clear facts of every known strike. On this conventional view the right to strike is simply the right of free men to withdraw their labour from undesired work (though some apologists concede that the withdrawal should not be in breach of contract). The alternative to this freedom to withdraw is forced labour, a mark of the condition of a serf, or slave, or conscript, or prisoner lawfully sentenced to the loss of his liberty.

However, the unqualified right to withdraw labour, which is a clear right of free men, does not describe the behaviour of strikers. Free workers would in effect say to employers: 'We refuse to work for you on present terms. Good-bye'; or perhaps, 'We refuse to work for you on present terms; but if you can agree with us on new terms satisfactory to us, we shall be ready to re-enter your employment. If not, good-bye'. Both employers and employees would then be free to test the market. If employers could hire substitute labour on terms more satisfactory to themselves than

[1] A. A. Alchian and W. R. Allen, *University Economics*, Wadsworth Publishing Co., California, 2nd Edn., 1967, p. 327.

[2] Morgan O. Reynolds, *Power and Privilege*, Universe Books, New York, 1984, pp. 48-49.

[10]

those demanded by their erstwhile employees, they would be free to do so without let or hindrance. If not, they might have to accept the terms required by their former employees and re-hire them; or they might wholly or partly resort to other expedients, such as substitution of machinery for labour, or the adoption of new processes, or even the abandonment of the trade concerned. Similarly, the withdrawing employees could seek other and better employment elsewhere. If they succeeded, they would thus demonstrate that their former employer's terms were below the free-market level. If they failed, they would be free to seek re-employment on the former terms or on any other terms agreeable to the employers. These are the obvious features of the rights of free men, whether employees or employers.

To describe the actual behaviour of strikers in this fashion would be to offer a travesty of the facts. Strikers, whether their strike be union-authorised or wild-cat, withdraw from the performance of their jobs, but in the only relevant sense they do not withdraw their labour. The jobs from which they have withdrawn performance belong to them, they maintain. Their labour is present and available for those jobs, and woe betide any other workers ('scabs', 'blacklegs', etc) who may seek to offer their labour in place of that of the strikers. Woe betide also any employer who seeks to hire the labour of such 'interlopers'. Throughout the history of unionism this has been the stance adopted by strikers, usually accompanied by loud oral abuse of employers and 'interlopers' at least and often also by attempted or actual physical violence. By contrast, on those infrequent occasions that employers have withdrawn their service from their employees by a lock-out, the welkin has rung with complaints against employer tyranny. If, further, the strikers were able to obtain more satisfactory jobs elsewhere, any employer action to prevent them from so doing would be universally and justly condemned as an utterly intolerable invasion of workers' freedom. In the past some employers have occasionally used blacklists to inhibit the employment of individual employees, though not of whole bodies of strikers,[1] but there has never been a counterpart by employers of the abuse

---

[1] Of course, many employers will not employ other firms' striking employees, but that is the result of their own assessment of the possible value to themselves of the strikers' labour, not of an invasion of the strikers' liberty.

and physical violence habitually vented against them and against 'interlopers' by strikers.[1]

Thus, whilst claiming liberty for themselves, strikers deny it to employers and 'interlopers'. If we were to describe the status which they offer employers as that of 'serfs', we should doubtless be met with loud cries of derision. Yet it would be a correct description. Serfs were not slaves. They had their rights in law. The essence of their condition was that they were tied to their lord and his land. So, too, strikers maintain that their employers are tied to them. However that condition may be described, it cannot be that of free men in a free society.

It may be urged that our law itself now binds the employer to the employee, at least in a manner making the contract of employment something like a marriage rather than a lord-serf relationship. It is true that the employee may obtain a divorce without cause and at any time (subject to due notice) simply by dismissing himself, but the employer may do so only on pain of payment of damages if he lacks good cause – that is, if the dismissal of the employee is judged to be 'unfair'. But this only indicates how far we have slipped from the principles and practices of a free society. In such a society an employment may be ended either according to contract or in breach of contract. In the former case, laws and rights have nothing further to say. In the latter case, damages may ensue. The concept of 'unfair dismissal', as distinct from breach of contract, is alien to the fundamental rights of free men. Whatever else it does, this regrettable development of our

---

[1] It has been often alleged and is widely believed that in the United States in the 19th and early 20th centuries, employers applied strong-arm methods (using the services of Pinkerton's men and the like) to impose a tyranny on their workers. This is a splendid example of the success of the Big Lie. First, the Pinkerton's men and their kind were always brought in for defence against intolerable union violence, not to put down peaceful workers (as just one example among many, in the infamous Homestead strike of 1892 the strikers brought up cannon to attack the employers' plant). In the long history of American labour conflict, the bombings, shootings, and hi-jackings have always been the work of unions, not of employers. The Hobbs Act, which makes such acts of physical violence a Federal offence and hence subject to the attentions of the FBI, a much more effective law enforcement body than State police or local sheriffs, was declared by the Supreme Court to be inapplicable in labour disputes (USA *v.* Enmons, 410 U.S. 396 (1973)), a licence to use violence of which the unions have taken eager advantage. Secondly, these defensive forces were not used to prevent strikers from obtaining employment elsewhere, though blacklists were in some cases.

labour law gives very little colour to strikers' demands that they, and they alone, are entitled to certain jobs simply because they have held them in the past. In by far the great majority of cases, the penalty on the employer for the 'unfair dismissal' of an employee is to pay compensation, not to reinstate him. The strikers' demand for an inalienable right to, and property in, a particular job cannot be made conformable to the principles of liberty under law for all. In pursuing our examination of the right to strike, it will be our purpose to find a right which does conform to those principles and no other.

Concept of 'unfair dismissal' retrograde

It should be understood that the concept of unfair dismissal is alien to the rights of free men only when it is imposed upon the employer by way of legal duty or liability. There can be no objection to the inclusion of provisions relating to unfair dismissal in contracts made voluntarily between employers and employees and/or their unions. It is obviously permissible for employers and employees and/or their unions to agree upon a system of grievance procedures, which might well include provision for some concept of unfair dismissal and for the payment of compensation if it arises. So, too, if an employer is prepared by voluntary agreement to endow his employee with any other kind of property in his job, he is clearly entitled to do so. Thus is illustrated the difference between human relationships based on contract and those based on status. It was once well understood that the progress of a free and civilised order lay forward from status to contract. It is a deplorable feature of our times that the thrust of much modern social and economic legislation is backward to the primitive principle of status. The imposition upon the employer of the concept of unfair dismissal by law, and outside the purview of voluntary contract, and similarly the endowment of the employee with some kind of property right in a job, are prime examples of this reversion to the governance of status.

The essential reason why the non-contractual claim to a property in a job is incompatible with the principles of liberty under law is that it cannot be generalised. The right to life, liberty and the pursuit of happiness (as in the American Declaration of Independence), or to life, liberty and property (as in the American Fifth

[13]

Amendment) can be vested in all persons simultaneously without harm to the right of any one of them. For example, one person's right to property extends only to the point where it co-exists with other persons' right to property; so too with the right of free worship, free speech, free assembly and the like. A right to a job or to a property in a job imposes a burden upon someone to supply the job or provide the property. It may be possible without contravention of this principle for a state to endow particular persons with some right at the state's expense, though this too has very dubious features, but to endow A with a right at the expense of B, who has committed no offence against A and broken no contract with him, must be a derogation from B's right to equality of liberty with everyone else.

Effects of unfair dismissal

Since the concept of unfair dismissal was embodied in our law, voices have been heard to declare that it has improved the behaviour of employers towards employees, that it has made them recognise the essential contribution of employees to the success of their business, and that this contribution should earn a dismissed employee due compensation. It would be difficult to find contentions with less substance.

First, the effect upon employers' behaviour has been to add to the influences which have given us the flabby manager, tolerant of indiscipline, who perhaps has been a major cause of Britain's relative economic, and absolute manufacturing, decline. This effect has not been apparent in recent years because by good fortune it has been more than counterbalanced by the effect on worker and union behaviour of the 1980-82-84 UK employment legislation[1] and of the cold economic climate which has at last overtaken managerial incompetence or weakness. Thus, happily, the flabby manager is departing our scene, but in spite of, not because of, burdens imposed on employers by unfair dismissal provisions among others.

Secondly, in a free labour market the full prospective value of the worker's contribution to the product of the enterprise is met by the wage. Where the worker's wage is influenced by the power

[1] The Employment Act, 1980; The Employment Act, 1982; The Trade Union Act, 1984.

[14]

of a union monopoly, it will be above the full value of his prospective contribution to the product unless the excess can be wholly passed on to the consumer. If the employer is a monopsonist – that is, a monopolistic purchaser of some type of labour – it is conceivable that the wage may be less than the worker's prospective contribution to the product, but this will be a short-term effect unless the worker has only one specific skill or ability and cannot acquire some new skill or ability. In any case, the monopsonist employer is almost certain to be met by a monopolist union, the two being likely to conspire happily against the consumer. Hence, as an almost universal rule, when the employer has paid the worker his wage, he owes him no more (unless he has voluntarily contracted to make an extra payment). Of course, the notion that somehow the wage is less than the value of the worker's work is deeply embedded in the public mind, not merely among those wedded to the Marxist surplus value superstition. This merely illustrates the depressing fact that two centuries of rational economic thought and analysis have failed to eradicate this, among other errors, from the public mind. What is especially deplorable is its influence upon the mind of many an otherwise educated person.

The public is often confused by the payment by a 'good' employer of more than the going rate for his jobs, concluding that other employers must therefore be exploiting their workers. But the purpose of the 'good' employer may be to attract the best workers, or to produce loyalty and contentment among his workers. He pays more, but if he knows what he is doing, what he gets is worth more. The employer who pays less because he is not seeking superior ability, or loyalty, or contentment, is still forced in a market that is regulated by competition to pay the full prospective value of the work.

The most harmful effect of the unfair dismissal liability, in common with other legislative attempts at so-called employment protection, is unemployment. All attempts at employment protection of this kind amount to contraception, still-birth, or abortion of jobs, especially contraception. Thus the wariness of the employer against hiring more workers for fear of the statutory burdens involved imposes its most deplorable effect upon the unemployed, the most disadvantaged of all in the labour market. This is often masked from view by the employer's substitution

[15]

of labour-saving equipment in place of additions to his work-force. The substitution of equipment for labour where equipment is more economic than labour in free competition with each other increases, not reduces, wealth and jobs, though the new jobs may be in other enterprises. But the substitution of equipment for labour because the employment of labour is hindered by some specially imposed disadvantage is retrograde, not progressive, a net *destroyer*, not creator, of wealth and jobs.

Light on the nature of a right to strike?

If, in searching for an elucidation of the nature of a right to strike, we turn to documents such as the United Nations' International Covenant on Civil and Political Rights, and the International Covenant on Economic, Social and Cultural Rights, or the European Convention on Human Rights and Fundamental Freedoms and the European Social Charter, we find that references to the right to strike are not accompanied by definitions. It appears to be assumed that the right to strike is a self-evident right, understood by all and therefore requiring no definition.

However, Article 7(4) of the European Social Charter does make a qualification of the right. It reads

'. . . the right of workers and employers to collective action in cases of conflicts of interest, including the right to strike, is subject to obligations that might arise out of collective agreements entered into'.

Notice that on this footing the right to strike is qualified only by obligations arising from collective agreements, not those arising from contractual agreements with or between individuals, which is a distinction difficult to justify. But the Committee of Experts, charged with the interpretation of the Charter, has taken the qualification further. It has construed the right to strike as arising only in conflicts of interests, not of other rights of the parties. Furthermore, it has concluded that the right to strike does not preclude the imposition under law of a 'cooling-off' period, or the prohibition of strikes in certain essential services, or the determination that illegal political strikes are outside the purview of collective bargaining.

In the United Kingdom legislation of 1980-82-84, the right to strike is constrained by the limitation on secondary action and

[16]

by the requirement of pre-authorisation by a ballot of the trade union members concerned. Doubtless these provisions have circumscribed the right to strike to an important degree. Nevertheless, where unions abide by them and are still able to strike lawfully, the attitude to employers and 'interlopers' described above as incompatible with the principles of liberty under law for all, still remains unchallenged by our law.

The legal consequences of a strike

In our law most contracts of employment may be lawfully terminated only on due notice on either side. The length of notice may be explicitly stated in the contract, or it may be inferred from the conduct of the parties or from the custom of the trade. If the length of notice is not stated and cannot be inferred, a period of at least a week is laid down by Section 49 of the Employment Protection (Consolidation) Act, 1978, where the employee has been employed for one month or more. The period of notice is not the same for employee and employer. The employee must give notice of not less than a week. The employer must give notice of not less than a week if the continuous employment has been for less than two years; of not less than one week for each year if the continuous employment has been for two to 12 years; and of not less than 12 weeks if the continuous employment has been for 12 years or more.

If a strike is called without the notice duly required for termination, though not contrary to the 1980-82-84 limitations, it is clearly a breach of contract and entitles the employer to damages (Russell *v.* Amalgamated Society of Carpenters;[1] Denaby and Cadeby Main Collieries *v.* Yorkshire Miners Association[2]). However, the employer's remedy does not lie against the union (unless this is clearly specified in the union agreement), since union agreements *per se* are not contractually enforceable. His remedy is therefore against the individual employees, which may be of little use to him. Indeed, even if the individual employees are worth powder and shot in a court action for damages, the employer may often judge such action to be unwise and counter-productive, especially if he hopes to have the strikers return to work on terms

[1] 1912 AC 421.   [2] 1906 AC 384.

[17]

satisfactory to himself. He may judge it wise to stay his hand even where he could take action against the union itself on grounds of statutory illegality or contempt of court. Not every employer entitled to use the provisions of the 1980-82-84 legislation against a union has chosen to do so.[1]

Suppose that the strike is called with due notice. Does this mean that the strikers have thereby terminated the contract of employment? We know very well that in their minds they have not. As we have noted, they consider the jobs still to be theirs. The matter is complicated by the fact that under Schedule 13(15) of the Employment Protection (Consolidation) Act, 1978, those statutory rights of an employee which depend upon continuity do not lapse by reason of a strike if the employee is re-hired after the strike. But, logically, the contractual rights of an employee should lapse on a strike as they would on a termination with due notice.

Lord Denning's judgements

Lord Denning considered this question in Stratford *v*. Lindley.[2] He said:

'Suppose that a trade union officer gives a strike notice. He says to an employer: "We are going to call a strike on Monday week unless you increase the men's wages by £1 a week" – or "unless you dismiss yonder man who is not a member of the union" – or "unless you cease

---

[1] Consider, for example, the 1984-85 miners' strike, when the National Coal Board refrained from taking the union to court (though others did so). It is for this reason that laws intended to restrain unions from illegal action are not always effective. Until President Reagan dismissed the illegally striking air traffic controllers in 1981, American unions were normally completely confident that no penalties would be imposed for an illegal strike where the employer was the Federal or a State Government or governmental authority. As the leader of PATCO, the air traffic controllers' union, assured his members, 'the only illegal strike is a failed strike'. What he meant was that when terms were settled for the end of the strike, the first requirement of the union would be a Presidential pardon for the illegality, and that such a pardon had always been granted. He and his members were thunderstruck when Mr Reagan refused to follow this practice. Similarly, New York State has a long-standing law (the Taylor Law) which makes strikes by public servants illegal. Yet public service unions have struck many times, especially in New York City, with impunity. On settlement the first agreed requirement has been a gubernatorial pardon (i.e. by the Governor of New York State).

[2] 1964 2AER 209; 1965 AC 285.

to deal with such and such a customer". Such a notice is not to be construed as if it were a week's notice on behalf of the men to terminate their employment, for that is the last thing any of the men would desire. They do not want to lose their pension rights and so forth by giving up their jobs. The strike notice is nothing more nor less than a notice that the men will not come to work. In short, that they will break their contracts".'

In support he quoted an observation by Lord Devlin in Rookes v. Barnard,[1] as follows:

'There is nothing to differentiate a threat of a breach of contract from a threat of physical violence or any other illegal threat. . . . The object of the notice of January 10 was not to terminate the contract after due notice or otherwise but to break it by withholding labour but keeping the contract alive.'

Thus in Lord Denning's view the notice to strike was not a notice to terminate the contract but merely a notice of an intention to break it. Hence the strike had to be treated in law as a breach of the contract, with such legal consequences as might follow a breach. A few years later, however, in Morgan v. Fry,[2] he changed his mind. He referred to his statement in Stratford v. Lindley, saying:

'It is difficult to see the logical flaw in that argument, but there must be something wrong with it; for if that argument were correct, it would do away with the right to strike in this country. It has been held for over sixty years that workmen have a right to strike (including therein a right to say that they will not work with non-unionists) provided that they give sufficient notice beforehand, and a notice is sufficient if it is at least as long as the notice to terminate the contract.'

In support he quoted Lord Evershed's dictum in Rookes v. Barnard:

'. . . it has long been recognised that strike action or threats of strike action . . . in the case of a trade dispute do not involve any wrongful action on the part of the employees, whose service contracts are not regarded as being or intended to be thereby terminated'.

Lord Evershed's dictum was, however, obiter and without compelling authority.

[1] 1964 AC 1129.   [2] 1968 2QB 210; 1968 3AER 452.

Regrettably, it has to be said that Lord Denning sadly misdirected himself in Morgan v. Fry. He was very close to the truth in Stratford v. Lindley, and had no need to retreat from his position therein, at least not for the reason he gave.

In construing the meaning of a contract it is normally correct to look to the intentions of the parties. However, in the case of strike action there is an awkward difficulty. The conscious intentions of the strikers are likely to be misleading because the strikers and their union leaders are not thinking in terms of law at all, or, if any element of law comes within their ken, they believe, and act as if, they are above it (especially if they regard it as 'Tory' law). Hence we must look, not to the strikers' conscious intentions, which are likely to be muddled and self-contradictory in law, but to the reasonable meaning or implication of what they do. When they give their strike notice, they do not consciously intend to repudiate the contract and thus to terminate it, but they do intend to repudiate its terms. Hence Lord Denning was right in Stratford v. Lindley to conclude that the strike notice was a notice to break the contract, giving rise in law to penalties for breach. But it was also a breach which amounted to a termination. Hence the employer would be entitled to treat the notice to strike as a notice to terminate accompanied by an offer to attempt to negotiate a new contract.

Lord Denning's regrettable 'erroneous belief'

What is especially regrettable in Lord Denning's change of mind in Morgan v. Fry is his erroneous belief that if he had been right in Stratford v. Lindley, the right to strike would be done away with. Of course, if the right to strike meant, as for generations we have allowed strikers and their leaders to think, that they could eat their cake and still have it, repudiate a contract's terms and yet keep it, withdraw performance of their jobs and yet retain them, the penalties arising on the Stratford v. Lindley principle would doubtless make such a strike unprofitable and ultimately do away with it. But this is not the only meaning to be attached to the right to strike, and it is astonishing that so eminent a judge as Lord Denning, and one who in his long years on the Bench often showed himself a watchful guardian of our liberties against some of the pretensions of organised labour, should have thought so.

If the right to strike meant the right simply to withdraw one's labour, and thus to test the labour market, the Stratford *v.* Lindley principle would not apply to it or deter it.

Concluding, in Morgan *v.* Fry, that the strike was neither breach nor termination, Lord Denning decided that it amounted only to a suspension of the contract, which thus remained in being though in a sort of temporary coma. But Lord Justice Davies dissented, holding that the notice to strike was a notice to terminate, with an offer to work on new terms. For the suspension of a contract must be agreed between the parties. It is not open to one contracting party to suspend a contract unilaterally. It is true that on the settlement of the strike, the employer may be prepared to treat the contract as if it had been suspended, but this is not the same as prior consent to suspension. Furthermore, the strike may never be settled. It may peter out as a failure, and the employer may be able to hire new and different labour. It may also be true that, from the outset, the employer thinks of the strike as suspension, not termination, because he hopes that the strikers will return to work with him at the end of the strike. In such a case, which doubtless is common, it may be said that there is indeed a consensual suspension.

This calls for the following observations. First, if the strike peters out as a failure and the employer can hire new labour, suspension will turn into termination whether the strikers think so or not. Second, the suspension cannot be truly consensual unless its acceptance is clearly signified by the employer or is clearly implied by his behaviour. The strike action alone cannot make it so. Third, and most important, the employer's hope of the return of the strikers may have been heavily conditioned by the conventional acceptance of the strikers' assertion of a property right in their jobs and of their 'right' to prevent the hiring of 'interlopers'. If a strike meant peaceful self-dismissal, the tendency of employers to think *ab initio* in terms of suspension, not termination, might well become exceptional. Furthermore, if the strike notice is only a notice to suspend, not to terminate, why should the period of notice have to be at least as long as the notice required for termination, as Lord Denning said it should in Morgan *v.* Fry? What is the relevance of the notice required for termination, if the case is not one of termination? Suppose that it was the employer who sought suspension. Would he have to give

[21]

notice varying from one to 12 weeks according to the various employees' length of service?

Go-slows, work-to-rule, and sit-ins

What about go-slows, work-to-rule, and sit-ins? A sit-in will be associated with a strike, but the go-slow and the work-to-rule are often used to produce something like the effect of a strike at little or no cost to the workers. A go-slow is patently a breach of contract, but a work-to-rule is on the face of it not a breach of contract but a punctilious observance of it. Fortunately, the law is not such an ass as to fail to see the true nature of what is often called a work-to-rule. Thus in Secretary of State for Employment v. ASLEF,[1] it was held to be a breach of contract to give the employer's rules an unreasonable construction (which is the case in many instances of supposed work-to-rule), and, further, a breach wilfully to obstruct the employer's business.

A sit-in is at least a tort (i.e. a civil wrong) and may also be a crime. Yet, if it happens to be practicable, it is widely regarded by strikers and their sympathisers as an element in a rightful strike. Where force was used or threatened, as it often has been, the case was subject until 1977 to certain ancient Forcible Entry Acts of Parliament of the 14th to the 17th centuries which made entry into possession of premises and maintenance of possession by the use or threat of force serious criminal offences; and as late as 1971, in Regina v. Robinson,[2] it was held that an indication by a sitter-in that any attempt to enter would be opposed by force might amount to forcible detainer under the ancient law even if the rightful owner, being deterred, made no effort to enter. These ancient Acts were repealed by the Criminal Law Act, 1977, by which provisions relating to industrial sit-ins became much more limited, as the Act was principally concerned with entry into and occupation of residential premises (the house 'squatter' problem). However, the law relating to factory breaking remains, and entry by illicit means combined with theft or other illicit acts within the premises would bring the sit-in within its ambit. The sit-in is surely a reprehensible practice, and it is a sad commentary on the prevailing tendency to turn a blind eye to

[1] 1972 2QB 443; 1972 2AER 853. [2] 1971 1QB 156; 1970 3AER 369.

wrongs committed by strikers that legal remedies against it are hardly ever applied.

Confusion on stilts

We have noted the deep confusion in the public mind about the proper or acceptable characteristics of the right to strike; and even the confusion in the minds of eminent judges about the nature and legal consequences of a strike. But there are other, and worse, confusions than these.

For nearly two centuries the legal status of trade unions has been shrouded in confusion. Before 1824, under the common law and the Combination Acts of 1799 and 1800, unions were illegal conspiracies in restraint of trade. After the passage of the Acts of Parliament of 1824[1] and 1825,[2] until 1871[3] they were no longer illegal organisations, but exactly what they were it is difficult to say. Their existence was of a shadowy kind, only just within the range of legality, but no-one could say positively what their status in law was. In particular, unions were incapable of making contracts establishing any legal rights for or against them, and their capacity to hold any property was very doubtful. Furthermore, though they were no longer *ipso facto* illegal bodies acting in restraint of trade, the hostility of the common law to restraint of trade and to tortious conspiracy remained intact, and therefore an ever-present danger to the unions. In the late 19th century it was qualified and attenuated by the Mogul Steamship[4] and Maxim Nordenfelt[5] cases, but by then the Act of 1871 had given the unions a more clear legality.

Thus the legal situation of the unions in this period was a hazardous and confused one. In contrast, this was the period

[1] Combination Laws Repeal Act, 1824.

[2] Combination Act, 1825.

[3] Trade Union Act, 1871.

[4] Mogul S.S. Co. *v.* McGregor Gow, 1889 2QBD 598; 1892 AC 25.

[5] Nordenfelt *v.* Maxim Nordenfelt, 1894 AC 535. The Mogul and Nordenfelt cases were concerned with restrictive practices by business companies, not trade unions. They held that such practices might not be unlawful restraints of trade if they were pursued for the normal and regular expansion or safeguarding of business, uncontaminated by an attempt or desire to harm or destroy other business firms.

when Parliament established clear foundations for the principle of limited liability for business companies, and set about the development of modern company law aimed at defining the constitutions of companies, the duties of directors, and the rights of shareholders and creditors.

As mentioned above, since the passage of the Trade Union Act of 1871, the status of the unions has unquestionably been fully legal. Yet there remain elements in it which to a lawyer must be confused and confusing. Save for the exceptional and very minor case of 'special register unions' (bodies corporate which are a relic of the legislation promoted by the Heath Government in 1972-74), a trade union is still not a legal entity existing separately from its members (unlike, for example, a business limited liability company). In legal theory, a union is a number of individuals described by a collective name. But as this would produce awkward difficulties in situations of importance both for their members and for employers and others with whom they have dealings, statutes have conferred some important attributes of legal personality upon them. Thus trade unions are now *sui generis*, somewhere between corporations and unincorporated associations of individuals. It is obviously a confusing situation, baffling to anyone who looks for logic or consistency in the law. In the fundamental matter of agreements with employers, we must note that collective bargains are not normally enforceable as contracts. There is a conclusive presumption that the parties intend no enforceability unless the agreement is in writing and expressly states that it, or part of it, is intended to be enforceable.[1] Even in this latter rare case, enforceability may fail on other grounds – for example, uncertainty, absence of consideration, illegality, and so on.

'A legal dog's breakfast'

The provisions of the Trade Union and Labour Relations Act, 1974, well display the lack of logic of this situation. Not only is a trade union not a corporation or a quasi-corporation, but it is also not to be treated as if it were a body corporate. Yet the Act also provides that a union can make contracts, hold property (vested in a trust), and can take legal proceedings (but, *per contra*, note

[1] Trade Union and Labour Relations Act, 1974, Section 18(1)(3).

[24]

the case of the EEPTU *v.* Times Newspapers,[1] where it was held that a union could not sue for libel for lack of sufficient personality). To use very colloquial language, it is not unfair to describe the state of trade union law as a legal dog's breakfast.[2] The unions love this situation. For the confusions and idiosyncrasies of trade union law make them feel in a sense outside the law and therefore above it. The commonest refrain in the union litany is 'Let the law leave us alone so that we can get on with free collective bargaining' (meaning bargaining by force where necessary).

How has this situation arisen? Because, among all social and economic institutions, in the case of the unions Parliament and the courts have uniquely relied upon the principle or device of immunities from the normal provisions of the law. It is an abdication from the true way by which legislatures and courts develop the legal status of social and economic institutions. In practice it produces doubt and confusion about the status of the institution concerned, and tends to confer upon it quasi-rights and powers

---

[1] 1980 1AER 1097.

[2] It is surely a rare branch of law which can display so remarkable confusion on a fundamental issue as that which prevailed from the 1870s to 1901 in labour law. In that period it was thought by all union leaders and most employers and lawyers that the combined effect of the Trade Union Act, 1871, and the Conspiracy and Protection of Property Act, 1875, had given the unions immunity against legal action for unlawful acts committed by their members in trade disputes. In the famous Taff Vale case of 1901 the House of Lords decided otherwise.

In most branches of law it is possible to find court decisions which are not easily reconcilable, but it is rare to find two cases, decided within a short period by the same court, so difficult to reconcile with each other as Allen *v.* Flood, 1898 AC 1, and Quinn *v.* Leathem, 1901 AC 495. Both were concerned with the question whether pressure by or for a union upon an employer to dismiss from his employment an employee who, being a non-member or for any other reason is in bad odour with the union, was actionable. The facts in these two cases were not all similar, but contradictory judgements resulted in them even on the facts which were indistinguishable from each other except perhaps, if at all, with Sam Weller's 'double hextra power gas microscope'. In Allen *v.* Flood the case was decided by a majority of six to three in a highly exceptional court of nine Law Lords (Lords of Appeal in Ordinary), with eight High Court judges in attendance to offer their opinions, who between them produced a marvellous display of judicial disagreement. To reach their decision the House of Lords majority had to reverse the decisions of both the court of first instance and the Court of Appeal.

Both cases have to be treated as good law by lawyers, who therefore have the task of reconciling them. It is a task demanding very exceptional ingenuity, if it can be done at all.

incompatible with the rule of law. It has been made very much worse by the lamentable Trade Disputes Act, 1906, and by succeeding Acts of Parliament which have extended the immunities to extraordinary lengths. It is true that the 1980-82-84 legislation has narrowed the powers which have thus been nurtured for the unions, but the principle of the immunities remains. As long as the unions respect the limits imposed by the 1980-82-84 legislation, the behaviour lawfully open to them remains protected by immunities.

It is not surprising that until recently the unions and their academic apologists were much enamoured with the system of immunities, for they expected that no other system would give them such power as they had. If anyone suggested that unions, like business companies under company law, should be given a charter of positive rights and duties, not negative immunities, union leaders and their apologists would rise in high dudgeon to denounce so infamous a proposal. Recently, some union apologists and perhaps a union leader or two have perceived a danger in reliance on a system of immunities, which the general public is beginning to find questionable. Hence a system of positive rights and duties may begin to find favour among the unions' political friends. We may be sure that such a system would not be acceptable to the unions unless it not only reproduced the effect of the immunities, but also removed the limitations put upon the immunities by the 1980-82-84 legislation.

Sources of confusion

When a system of law has over a long period become as confused as our law relating to unions and strikes, the reasons are sure to lie in the grip of one or more errors, myths or superstitions on the public mind. Furthermore, one is likely to find that the erroneous ideas have a grip not only on the minds of the masses, but also on the minds of a considerable number of men of learning and intelligence (as did the belief in witches and witchcraft in the 16th and 17th centuries). Indeed, without the latter, these ideas could not maintain their sway for a long time. So it has been in this case.

The most powerful of these erroneous ideas has been the belief that the bargaining power of the individual worker is weak while that of the employer is strong. Hence the worker appears to need the union to even the balance.

Consider the following statement by Professor Cyril Grunfeld, a noted scholar in the field of labour law:

'Essentially it is only the ultimate power of union officials and their rank-and-file members to disrupt production, services, or the conduct of an enterprise by the withdrawal of labour which prevents even the most enlightened managerial régime from becoming mere paternalism.

'The law governing strikes and other forms of direct action is the law which enables union officials to carry out their vitally important work in the conduct of labour-management relations by enabling them to meet management on approximately equal terms; in other words, the law governing strikes is the law that regulates the balance of industrial power, which underlies the entire contemporary structure of voluntary collective negotiation and consultation.'[1]

To this a footnote is added:

'The statement in the text is made in the belief that, if one set of human beings is placed in a position of unchecked industrial authority over another set of human beings, to expect the former to keep the interests of the latter constantly in mind and, for example, to increase the latter's earnings as soon as the surplus becomes available and in the fullest equitable measure, is to place on human nature a strain it was never designed to bear.'

Consider another statement from a leading compendium of labour law:

'The law of labour relations in this country is based upon the principle of free collective bargaining. The argument runs thus. It is the function of law to maintain a fair balance between competing interests in society. The relationship between employer and employed is inherently one of imbalance: the employer is in a superior economic position and the employee in an inferior one so that within limits the employer can dictate the terms of employment to the employee, and so exploit him. Therefore the law should intervene to protect the employee against such exploitation and redress the balance.'[2]

[1] Cyril Grunfeld, *Modern Trade Union Law*, Sweet and Maxwell, London, 1966, pp. 317-318.

[2] *Harvey on Industrial Relations and Employment Law*, Part V, para. 1, Butterworths, November 1985.

In these statements there is regrettably no understanding of the nature of a free market. The employer is entirely exempt, apparently, from the constraints of the market, so that the only constraint possible is that of union power. It is a striking example of the decline of understanding of how free markets work which is typical of our times, even among scholarly men. These views are very powerful because they appear to be so obviously true to those unschooled in the nature of free markets. Few feel a need to subject them to analysis or to test them against the relevant facts. Picture the individual worker as poor and weak and the employer as rich and strong, and it seems as if these views cannot be challenged. In truth they are false through and through. They cannot pass the tests of fact and analysis. Their apparently obvious truth makes them acceptable but does not substantiate them. So, too, our ancestors thought that the flatness of the earth and the geo-centricity of the solar system were so obviously confirmed by the senses as to be beyond challenge. Scholar of distinction though he is, Professor Grunfeld and all others who think that the worker would be at the mercy of the employer without the power of a union behind him are in this context Flat Earthers.[1]

---

[1] A remarkable example of this is displayed by Lord Scarman in *Trade Unions: Public Goods or Public 'Bads'?*, IEA Readings No. 17, Institute of Economic Affairs, 1978, p. 67, where he averred that '. . . the individual in our society, unless he organises with others, is helpless'. Thus the temporary typists and secretaries, gardeners, odd-job men, charladies, and the butlers, valets, and ladies' maids serving the rare few who can afford them, who have all made great gains in remuneration in our times, must suffer from a very peculiar helplessness.

PART II

THE THEORY OF THE WORKER'S BARGAINING DISADVANTAGE

IT IS now 56 years since Professor W. H. Hutt published his classic *The Theory of Collective Bargaining*.[1] Patiently, painstakingly and perceptively, he examined the theory of the worker's supposed bargaining disadvantage and gave it burial. It is a deplorable feature of our times that, except among economists, his work has passed over the heads not only of most in the general public but also of others who ought to know better. The truth is that there is no inherent employee bargaining disadvantage in a free labour market. In some cases the employer has an advantage and in others the employee has it. *But this is about a trend line of earnings and working conditions which, in a free labour market,*

---

[1] W. H. Hutt, *The Theory of Collective Bargaining*, P. S. King, London, 1930. In 1975 the Institute of Economic Affairs republished this seminal work, under the title *The Theory of Collective Bargaining, 1930-1975* (Hobart Paperback No. 8), in which Professor Hutt added a review of his analysis and conclusions in the light of the experience of the 45 years since the first publication. His original conclusions were unscathed, indeed reinforced, by that experience.

An illuminating illustration of the strength of the belief in the worker's bargaining disadvantage is given by Professor Hutt in the following extract from his book (p. 8):

'Even the supposed enemies of unions had often absorbed the typical belief in their (i.e. the unions') beneficence. Sheriff Alison, detested by the unions for his stern suppression of the disorders of the famous Glasgow cotton spinners' strike of 1838, gave evidence (before the Parliamentary Enquiry on Combinations, 1838) to the effect that workmen's combinations enabled the members to a certain degree to compensate and to enter with equality into the lists with capital; and by 1866, as Sir Archibald Alison, his views had not changed. "Without combinations", he said, "competition would force wages down and workers would be reduced to the condition of serfs in Russia or the Ryots of Hindostan".'

Of course it is very common to find businessmen and others who think that they believe in the principles of capitalism, but whose minds harbour myths and superstitions about capitalism which have been propagated by their enemies. It is a rare businessman who not only believes in capitalism but also understands it. And why not? They are not economists or philosophers and are almost as likely to absorb popular economic notions as other people.

[29]

is upward for the employee. Thus over time, and subject to the fluctuations of business cycles, it is the employee who has the relative advantage. For in a free market the trend of remuneration is upward for the average labour unit (say, hour, day or week), but not for each unit of capital. The rate of return for each unit of capital may fall to, and remain stable at, a low level (*cf.* the low rates of interest in prosperous Victorian times). In a free market, capitalists prosper not by a rise in the remuneration of each unit of capital but by the increase and accumulation of capital. This is why in every known case of a labour market which has been allowed to be free, the earnings and working conditions of labour have improved, not deteriorated. It is why the German Marxist Revisionists had to concede at the end of the 19th century that the Marxist theory of the immiseration of the proletariat had been shown by the facts to be untrue; and they knew that the gains of the German working class were not the product of union action. There are numerous other examples which are obvious to those who are prepared to see them.

Consider, for example, Hong Kong. Its labour market is as free as any can be, and unions there are insignificant. In 1945, the population was about 600,000, down by about a half from the pre-war figure, and most of them were starving and in rags because the Japanese had taken away almost everything of value which was moveable. Since then a flood of refugees has come from mainland China, also with nothing except intelligence and a will to work, so that the population has multiplied about nine times since 1945. Nowhere in the world could one find a situation closer to perfection for the grinding down of the worker by utterly preponderant employer power, if the theory of labour's built-in bargaining disadvantage were true. In fact the earnings of the Hong Kong workers have risen by a factor so high that no British union leader would even dream of claiming a comparable percentage rise for his members, not even those in the print unions who in the past have obtained massive increases by force and disruption.

Hutt's analysis

However, while theory may not be decisive unless confirmed by fact, it is also true that fact alone without theory may be a deceptive guide.[1] Hence we must turn to Professor Hutt's examination of the theory of the supposed bargaining disadvantage of the worker. In brief summary it is as follows.

First, in the early and middle years of the 19th century the Wage Fund theory seemed to show that unions could not raise wages generally. For it was thought that at any given time there was a limited amount available for the payment of the wage total, so that gains by some workers could be obtained only at the expense of other workers. The demise of the Wage Fund theory suggested to some that this impediment to union bargaining success had been shown to be non-existent. However, this was a misunderstanding. There were economists who believed in both the Wage Fund theory and in the theory of the individual worker's bargaining disadvantage, and there were others who disbelieved both. Doubts about the power of unions to raise wages never depended on the discredited Wage Fund theory.

The worker's 'lack-of-reserve' argument

Secondly, the worker was thought to suffer disadvantage because he had no reserve such as the employer had. Hence the worker's need was more immediate than the employer's and obliged him to accept whatever bargain was on offer while the employer could hold off for some time. This picture of relative bargaining power appears persuasive until examined.

In the first place, it is a long time since any significant number of workers were so close to bare subsistence as to have no power at all to pick and choose between jobs. Long before state unemployment benefit brought its own cushion to the out-of-work, it was a commonplace that workers with any skill would not accept an unskilled job simply because it was the first on offer, even if it happened to carry a skilled job's rate of wages. Nor would the unskilled themselves accept the first job on offer if it did not measure up to their accustomed expectations. The reason was clear. They did have reserves of one kind or another.

In the second place, the notion that employers had superior power to hold off bargaining was hardly persuasive. Many an

---

[1] As Goethe said: 'Das Höchste wäre zu begreifen dass alles Faktische schon Theorie ist' ('the most important thing to understand is that everything factual is already theory').

employer with a bank overdraft, bills to be settled for materials and equipment, and customers ready to go elsewhere if deliveries were behind time, would have been astonished to learn that he could hold off from hiring labour if he could not get it at his preferred price. Nor is the giant company, whose bargaining power is generally assumed to be vastly superior to that of the worker, necessarily better placed. Large and expensive plant, especially if production is by continuous process, makes an imperative demand for manning on pain of severe loss if it is not met.

In the third place, the argument based on the worker's presumed lack of reserve is flatly controverted by the regular worker's own objection to the 'pin-money' worker (a notable feature of the labour market when Professor Hutt was writing), who was ready to accept a lower wage precisely because she (always presumed to be a female; hence the 'pin-money' description) did have a reserve.

Labour a 'perishable commodity'

Associated with the 'lack-of-reserve' argument was the 'perishable commodity' argument. Labour, it was said, was 'perishable'; like cut flowers, it would not keep. If the worker withheld Monday's labour, he inevitably lost Monday's time. He could not recover it on Tuesday, for Tuesday's time belonged to that day, and could not be stretched to make up for Monday's time.

The 'perishable commodity' argument survives examination no better than the 'lack-of-reserve' argument. In the first place, it fastens attention to units of time as such, not to the value of that time to the worker. Of course, it is true that Monday's 24 hours are gone forever when Tuesday begins. But what matters is the value of the work which the worker might have done on Monday. Why cannot he recover it by working overtime on Tuesday, or Wednesday, or Thursday . . .? If he has a sufficient reserve to survive Monday without income, he may well calculate that he can make it up by exerting pressure on the employer to improve his terms, and even obtain overtime rates after Monday to make up for that day's lost work, thus scoring a double gain. Both workers and employers are well acquainted with this kind of ploy. Of course, the worker must use it with circumspection. If he holds off from work not only on Monday but for week after week after week, he may never recover the value of the working time thus thrown away. This, too, is a well-known experience, as the miners' strike most recently reminded us.

In the second place, the employer's time is also perishable. If he cannot employ his capital on Monday, he also loses the value of Monday's time. Of course, he may make it up by more intensive use of his capital subsequently. If the worker has to make good the reserve which he used to maintain himself on Monday, the employer has to make good the overhead cost which he lost on that day. He may be able to meet this cost better than his workers, but there are many cases where he is much less able to do so.

Presumed indeterminateness of the wage-rate

A more plausible explanation of the individual worker's supposed bargaining disadvantage seemed to lie in the presumed indeterminateness of the labour price or wage-rate. Indeterminateness meant that at any given quantity of supply and demand the market-clearing price was not a particular figure (as in conventional free-market supply and demand analysis) but within a range of prices. The individual worker is likely to be unaware of this range or its extent, or, if aware of it, insufficiently skilled in bargaining to take advantage of it. Therefore a union could raise his wage by using its marketing knowledge to secure a price near the top of the range.

There is both truth and error in this proposition. Where a commodity is homogeneous – for example, a particular grade of wheat, coffee, cocoa, tin, lead, rubber, etc. – and where market information is spread widely and rapidly, then at any given moment the market-clearing price is decidedly not indeterminate. Where a commodity is not homogeneous, the market-clearing price for each perceived type or grade will still be determinate, unless the spread of information among buyers and sellers is imperfect or the supply-demand situation varies from locality to locality and there are impediments, by way of costs or otherwise, to movement between localities. In the form that the indeterminateness of wages was mainly presented, it was in error. For it suggested that the market-clearing price was indeterminate in all cases because the employer was prepared to pay a wage somewhere within a range, if necessary at the expense of his capital. This was simply a misunderstanding of the operation of a free market.

[33]

But in the form which took account of the heterogeneity of labour, not only between grades but also within grades (no two workers are as alike as two bushels of a grade of wheat), and of impediments to geographical movement, the theory of indeterminateness had substance.

Unions can raise worker's bargaining power

It follows that in principle a union may be able to raise the worker's bargaining power. But such a union would be a market service organisation, using knowledge and skill without need for force or monopoly power. It would be a legitimate element in a free labour market. If it advised its members to withdraw their labour, it would be to test the market, not to assert a 'freehold' interest in the relinquished jobs, still less to back the claim with force or violence. It would be very different in character from the unions familiar to us, which seek to raise wages by asserting monopoly power, not by improving the efficiency of market pricing.

But if monopoly can help unions raise the workers' bargaining power, why should their members refrain from organising to exclude competition? We must follow through the effects of the use of a union's monopolistic power. Suppose that a powerful union secures a significant rise in its members' wages which raises costs to the employers above a free-market level. Who pays the bill? Not the employers to the extent that they can pass on the cost to others in prices or lower quality. Nor those to whom the cost is first passed to the extent that they can pass it to yet others. In this process of beggar-my-neighbour all we can say with certainty is that the cost will fall in various shares on the employers, suppliers of other factors of production, consumers, workers in other industries as well as some of the union members themselves in the industry where the process started, whose jobs the employers find it necessary to dispense with.

But this is in the short run. As time goes by the cost will be shifted more and more onto consumers and workers (including union members in both capacities); and the burden on capital will get less and less. This is because in broad terms only captive capital – that is, capital already invested and not moveable – can be exploited by the union squeeze. Capital not yet invested, or if

[34]

invested capable of being moved, cannot be so treated unless its owners have some non-economic reason to submit to the squeeze.[1] A union powerful enough to squeeze the capital in any industry unwittingly puts out a notice to non-captive capital: 'Keep out! Go elsewhere!'.

Thus in due time, which may be long indeed but also may be quite short, the powerful union's members find their industry and their jobs caught in a process of contraction. Furthermore, the union members in the ABC industry will not only in due time pay some cost for their union's squeeze on captive capital, but they will also pay the cost passed on to them as a result of the exactions of the powerful union in the XYZ industry. While each union instinctively stands shoulder to shoulder with all other unions, each respecting the others' picket lines, the world of powerful monopolistic unions is in practice plagued by a war of all against all, even though the warriors do not know it. The typical union belief that the free market is a jungle in which the strong batten on the weak is untrue. It is the world of powerful monopolistic unions which is a jungle.

So it is that in due time the monopolistic unions' members themselves come to be worse off than they would have been in a free labour market. That is why a country like Britain, whose labour market is dominated by powerful monopolistic unions, eventually falls behind countries whose labour markets are relatively free.

Other false ideas about union power

There are other erroneous ideas about the supposed benefit to workers of union power which have considerable influence on the public mind, though less than that concerned with relative bargaining power. Thus many have been told, and some believe, that unions are valuable to the worker (and also to the employer) because they raise the worker's productivity. There are indeed a

[1] In the highly exceptional case of Fleet Street, the social and political attractions of becoming a Press Baron have for many years induced rich men to throw new capital into the extraordinary captivity imposed by the print unions. But the mills of God, which may or may not grind slowly, do grind exceeding small. Hence the Fleet Street captivity is reaching its end. So too the captivity which taxpayers have allowed their capital to fall into at the hands of unions in nationalised industries appears to be not far off its end.

[35]

few cases where this does happen, but at least in the medium or long term any such productivity gains are more than offset by the depressing effects of other features of union action upon productivity. In the majority of cases it does not happen at all.[1]

Moreover, many have been told and believe that, whatever effect, beneficial or otherwise, unions may have on wages or conditions of work, they do protect the worker's human dignity. Wages and physical conditions are not everything. Human labour is not simply a market commodity to be sold and bought like shoes, or ships, or sealing wax, but something with a dignity of its own which deserves to be treated with respect. To ensure this respect is a task, it is thought, which the union is *par excellence* qualified to perform.

This belief is false on two counts. First, where unions have not been backed by legal privilege or governmental support, or have not been able to recruit members by violence, only a minority of workers join them. In the United States in 1930, only about 8 per cent of the labour force was in unions.[2] In Britain before the passage of the Trades Disputes Act, 1906, it was about 14 per cent. Did the vast majority of workers, who were not unionised, care nothing for their human dignity? Secondly, it is not true that human dignity plays no part in the free market for labour. One has only to think of domestic servants who were hardly ever

---

[1] For an effective refutation of the contention that unions raise productivity, Morgan O. Reynolds, *Power and Privilege, op. cit.*, pp. 83-88.

[2] It is sure to be contended by some that the low figure of union membership in the United States before the passage of the Norris-La Guardia Act, 1932, was caused by the bias of the law and courts against unions, shown especially by the frequent use of the injunction against union action. This was the burden of the very influential book, *The Labor Injunction*, by Frankfurter and Greene (Felix Frankfurter was then a Professor at the Harvard Law School and later became a Justice of the Supreme Court). It was mainly the influence of this book which caused Congress to enact the Norris-La Guardia Act which effectively terminated the use of the labour injunction and gave a great boost to union power.

The use of the injunction before 1932 has been examined with immense care and thoroughness by Professor Petro, who has shown conclusively that its use was not inspired by anti-union or anti-labour bias, but was based on the correct, impartial and traditional principles of the Anglo-American system of equity (in the Anglo-American legal system the injunction is an 'equitable remedy'). (Sylvester Petro, 'Injunctions and Labor Disputes, 1880-1932', *Wake Forest Law Review*, June 1978, pp. 341-576.) Professor Petro is careful not to say so, but it is fair to say that one may have doubts about the freedom of the Frankfurter-Greene book from unscholarly political bias.

unionised, but who about a half-century ago began to leave such service in droves because there was a flavour in it which they thought damaging to their dignity. Three hundred years ago Samuel Pepys wrote down a complaint that he had to raise his cook's wages because she demanded it *or would leave* (a clear benefit of a free market), and not long afterwards Daniel Defoe made a similar complaint about the rising demands of domestic servants which had to be met.[1] The fact is that it was free-market capitalism which first truly emancipated the worker from the multiple indignities which had been visited upon him for many centuries.

Does all this mean that unions harm rather than benefit the workers, and ought therefore to be disbanded *in their interests* (as well as in the interests of the whole society)? It would, if unions had to be bodies of the kind which are familiar to us, with the powers which are tolerated by us. But they do not have to be of this kind; and some countries are blessed with unions which are at least partially of a different kind. In Britain itself the electricians' union has made some progress towards aims and policies which will truly benefit its members and lead it away from our traditional union type, though it has a long way to go before reaching that desirable end.

What unions can do truly to benefit their members without detriment to others is well stated in the economics textbook from which we have already quoted:

'What the union can do in that respect is help that system (i.e. the free economy) to organise diverse talents more efficiently by smooth-

---

[1] Quoted in Professor Hutt's *The Theory of Collective Bargaining* (p. 33) as follows:

'And Defoe in 1725 deplored the fact that "women servants are now so scarce that . . . their wages are of late increased to six, seven, nay eight pounds per annum and upwards. . . . But the greatest abuse of all is that these creatures are become their own lawgivers; they hire themselves to you by their own will. That is a month's wages or a month's warning".'

These complaints show not only that domestic servants had acquired considerable bargaining power but also that they were in a position to expect respect for their human dignity. In those days it was lawful for employers to mete out physical chastisement to their domestic servants (and to their wives – John Milton found it not seldom necessary to beat his wife), but we may be sure that if Pepys or Defoe had done this they would soon have found themselves either with the dregs of the servant labour supply or with no servants at all (wives were less free than servants!).

ing grievance procedures, providing increased information about job opportunities, helping workers to improve their skills, and providing facilities for joint purchases (e.g. of insurance, loan services, etc.)'.[1]

Unions of this kind would enjoy a right to strike resting on rational foundations. The strike would be an element in the testing of the market. It would mean self-dismissal, but a self-dismissal calculated to bring the realities of the market clearly before the eyes of both employers and employees. We can now proceed to consider a programme for reform which would bring the unions into such a system.

[1] Alchian and Allen, *op. cit.*, p. 389.

PART III

A PROGRAMME FOR REFORM

Comparison with a capitalist cartel

CONSIDER A typical business cartel. For example, a group of gadget manufacturers agrees to fix the price of gadgets. In the United States this would be an unlawful, indeed criminal, act. In some other countries it would be lawful. In yet others it would be lawful or unlawful according to particular features of the agreement or of the industry.

Notice that so far in this example the manufacturers have done nothing other than fix prices. They have not required all gadget manufacturers to join their group, though they may well have invited them to do so; still less have they used or threatened violence to force dissident manufacturers into their group. They may decide not to make the agreement at all unless all the manufacturers join the group, but if they do decide to proceed with it without 100 per cent membership, they must put up peacefully with whatever degree of dissidence there is. Similarly, if one of the parties breaks the agreement they must put up with the situation peacefully, though in some circumstances in some jurisdictions they may be able to go to court to obtain either an injunction against the breach or damages for it. Of course, peaceful behaviour does not exclude the use of market power to achieve one's ends, except when the end – in this case the concerted fixing of prices – is unlawful. In those jurisdictions where it is lawful, the cartellists must rely solely upon their peaceful market power, and the issue as between them and any dissidents will depend upon the relative strength of their respective market powers.

If buyers seek to elude the group's grip by finding new sources of gadgets, or by resorting to substitutes for gadgets, the cartellists will not use violence to prevent them from doing so. They may seek to tie up alternative supplies or substitutes so that the buyers will not succeed in obtaining them, but the means for so doing will be peaceful. If, having agreed to sell gadgets at, say, £100 each

[39]

they decide at a later date to charge £110, they will terminate the first agreement by whatever notice is required and seek a new sales agreement with the buyers. They will do whatever they can peacefully to induce the buyers to buy from them and them only, but they will not claim that, once a buyer has made his first purchase agreement with them, he is tied to them as long as he remains in business.[1] It follows that if, in the first agreement, incidental benefits accrue to them in addition to the £100, they may seek to include them in a new agreement with the £110 price, but they will not claim that these incidental benefits are sacrosanct and therefore accrue to them while there is no agreement between them and the buyers. Here, again, the outcome will depend upon the relative strength of the peaceful market powers of the sellers and buyers.

Anti-trust

Suppose that trade unions were cartels of exactly this pattern. What would then be their legal status? In the United States, as we have noted, business cartels are unlawful. There is much to be said for such a position – indeed, it is cogently arguable that this part of American anti-trust law, Section 1 of the Sherman Act, is the *only* part of the whole corpus of that law (Sherman, Clayton, FTC Act, etc.) for which a fair case can be made. But there is also much to be said against that position. In actual operation, the record of Sherman, Section 1, has at best been mixed. Indeed, it can be argued that, even if it is assumed that cartels are inherently undesirable, anti-cartel laws are unnecessary because (*a*) all known persistently harmful cartels (and other limitations to competition) are the product of state blessing, protection and support, and (*b*) in the absence of such state favour private cartels have a natural tendency to collapse. Hence there is a strong case for Professor Hayek's view of many years that all that is necessary and desirable is that cartel agreements should not be enforceable at law.

In the early years of American anti-trust the law was held to apply to unions as well as to business cartels, but not with complete certainty or clarity. In 1914 the Clayton Act exempted

---

[1] Of course, they may seek to tie him by special rebates which he will lose if he buys from other suppliers, but this will be a peaceful arrangement.

unions from the main thrust of anti-trust, and in 1932 the Norris-La Guardia Act locked, barred and bolted the gates to protect them against anti-trust attack, except where they may be a collusive party to a business cartel. The reason for the exemption was the false assertion that labour was not an article of commerce, and later the law turned to strong positive support and privilege for unions in the Wagner Act, 1935, only partially redressed by the Taft-Hartley Act, 1947, and the Landrum-Griffin Act, 1959. In other principal jurisdictions it is taken for granted that unions are not to be treated as similar to business cartels, mainly on the view, already exposed, that without them the workers would be at the mercy of capitalist power.

The Hayekian principle

We may scorn the prevailing reasons for exempting unions from anti-trust and still take the view that, if unions were in fact of the same character as the peaceful business cartel described above, laws against them would be undesirable. If the Hayekian principle of the simple legal unenforceability of cartel agreements is right for business, it is equally right for labour. Of course, the absence of legal action against unions would have to be matched by the equal absence of state or legal action in their favour.

The Hayekian case for legal neutrality would possibly be even stronger in relation to peaceful labour than in relation to similar business cartels. For the likelihood is that most unions of such a character would have a chequered and ineffective career. They would negotiate with employers for their members, but every time they withdrew their labour in a dispute, their members would dismiss themselves from their jobs. They would be entitled to seek 100 per cent membership (i.e. a closed shop) by peaceful agreement, but employers would be equally entitled to make union membership a bar to employment (i.e. the 'yellow-dog' contract in American parlance). They would take no action except peaceful persuasion (not persuasion under threat of violence) against competing non-members ('scabs' or 'blacklegs'). In these circumstances, if unions were to retain their present character to some extent, possibly only unions of small numbers of men possessing exceptional and hard-to-substitute skills would be likely to be effective – and this only in the short or medium term,

[41]

for in the long term no skill is irreplaceable, and the very effectiveness of the unions would stimulate devices to dispense with their members' labour. Possibly also coal miners' unions might be effective, because miners tend to live in isolated, tightly-knit communities and because there are numerous occasions for disputes in their industry (*cf.* the persistence of effective collective action by the Asturian miners during General Franco's rule in Spain). However, even this is doubtful, for despite all its legal privileges and its constant resort to cruel violence, the United Mine-Workers' union has been unable to kill off the non-union mines in the United States. But if unions changed their character to conform with the rule of law and the requirements of the free market so as to become true service organisations for their members, then they could have a permanent and valuable role.

Obviously, unions in our world are not cartels of the peaceful business kind. What then are they? Before this question is answered, it is well to consider certain widespread beliefs which sustain the view that the unions familiar to us are worthy and necessary bodies.

Claims for the unions

First, unions are said to rest upon the fundamental right of association of free men in a free society. We need spend little time on this contention. Obviously, the right of association depends upon the association's purposes or practices. Associations whose acts or purposes are unlawful are called conspiracies and are proscribed. If it is judged that the purposes or practices of modern unions, though now lawful, ought to be made unlawful, they cannot be saved by appeal to a fundamental right of association.

Secondly, we are constantly told that the most characteristic and powerful instrument of union policy, namely the strike, is an expression of the fundamental right of free men to withdraw their labour. We have sought above to demonstrate the falsehood of this claim.

Thirdly, unions claim a right in justice to require membership as a condition of employment (the closed shop), or at least payment by non-members of dues equal to those levied upon members (the agency shop), because otherwise non-members would get the benefit of union action without paying for it (the 'free-rider' problem). This contention has little substance. In the first place, workers of above-average quality would get higher wages were it not for the uniformities imposed by union action. In the second place, union wage-rates are often no more than what would be established in a free market. In the third place, a non-member might claim with abundant reason that beyond the short term the effect of union power is to reduce employment and wages by way of its deterrent to investment and enterprise.

Threats, violence and power

The unions' own claims for a rationale for their actions are easily punctured. What the unions do not declare to the world is the crucial feature of their operations, namely violence or the threat of it. The threat is much more important than the actuality, for the threat operates at all times whereas the actuality displays itself only sporadically. It is a rare union, and usually only one which is also in some measure a professional association adhering to professional standards of behaviour, which does not rely on the threat of violence. This has been the case throughout union history; the difference between the moderate, responsible, or business-type of union and the revolutionary type is only a matter of degree. All known picketing has some element of the threat of violence in it. All sit-ins, however apparently peaceful, are unlawful seizures of employers' property. Signals of displeasure with individual members by shop stewards or other union agents or officials are read by those members as carrying some hint of violence, however minimal.

These observations on union claims confirm and emphasise the truth that unions differ fundamentally from the type of business cartel described above.Yet, if they are envisaged simply as cartels with illicit or undesirable modes of operation, an essential feature of their character is missed. The truth is that they are power structures, and the maintenance and expansion of power become more and more their purpose, irrespective of benefit or detriment to their members. By way of promise of benefit to their members they first climb on the worker's back, and from that coign of vantage they seek to climb upon the back of the whole society. Thus they become a state within the state, with a claim of right to the use of force upon the citizens which ought to be the monopoly of the state. Just as the citizen finds himself born subject to the rule of a state, without choice except by way of emigration, so the modern worker often finds himself willy-nilly subject in large measure to the power of some union if he wishes to earn a living. Accordingly, unless checked by law or popular resistance, the purpose of union leadership becomes less and less to render service to members and more and more to dominate them. The members become foot-soldiers, who are largely conscripted and must obey their officers, in an army which is used for aggression against the whole of society. This is why unions tend conspicuously to be undemocratic bodies, even in those cases where there are formally democratic procedures, and even though theoretically every conscript in the union army may carry a marshal's baton in his knapsack.[1]

A legal existence for unions

It follows that modern unionism in its typical form is a challenge to the authority of the state, and in particular an affront to the rule of law upon which the authority of the liberal state should rest. Hence, if unions were bound by their nature to assume the predominant character of modern unionism, the proper role of law would be to proscribe them. Whether their proscription *could in practice be enforced* is a separate question.

However, unless it is judged desirable to proscribe cartels of

[1] This view may be challenged on the ground that, especially in Britain, wildcat strikes have been common, thus demonstrating that union members are not subordinate to their leaders. This is a misunderstanding. In the first place, the wildcat strike itself rests upon the power of the union. Suppose that an employer sought to apply punitive measures against wildcat strikers. The union would rush to their defence, and the strikers could count on this. In the second place, if wildcat strikes erupt frequently, it means only that authority in the union army is dispersed. The individual member then fears the local non-commissioned officer (e.g. the British shop steward) as much as or more than the commissioned officers. He remains effectively an obedient conscripted foot-soldier.

This view may also be challenged now on the ground that the British legislation of 1980-82-84 has restored the unions to their members. So it has, in fair measure, with compulsory ballots for strikes and for the election of executive officers. But the power-seeking leaders have by no means given up, and they still have many strings to their bows. They will make their exit only when unions are forced by law to reconstitute themselves as voluntary service organisations for the true service of their members.

all kinds – a view which has been rejected above – it is unnecessary to have recourse to proscription. The purpose of law should then be to limit the activities of unions to those which would be pursued by completely peaceful cartels relying solely on market power.

Here we must admit a difficulty. Our gadget cartel would not be recognised in law at all, even though tolerated. It could own no property, nor could it sue or be sued as a corporate body. In the union case this would not be satisfactory, since it would be desirable to enable unions to hold property and to sue in contract and tort. The solution is to allow unions a legal corporate existence, but to make membership agreements unenforceable at law, and to subject union activities to such rules as would force them to be peaceful. The essentials of law and policy would then comprehend at least the following.

PROPOSALS

1. The law of tort should apply to unions and their members equally with all other bodies and persons. The exemption from liability in tort, which was given to British unions in 1906 and which has since then been partly extended, though also partly limited, is a flagrant breach of the rule of law, and has been a major cause of the lawless union power which has plagued Britain.

2. The law of contract should apply to unions and their members equally with all other bodies and persons (save that membership agreements should be unenforceable at law). Agreements between employers and unions should be fully enforceable against employers, unions, and individual union members by way of injunctions and awards of damages. If a union agreement is broken by individual members without the authority or connivance of the union, the employer should have a right of action not only against those members but also against the union unless its rules provide for the expulsion of members in breach of its agreements and the employer has prior notice of such rules.

3. All workers should be free in law to join or not to join a union, except that in certain specified cases such as, for example, the

police, prison warders, firemen, public health personnel, higher civil servants, and possibly others, it may be a justifiable act of public prudence, to be decided on its merits in each case, to forbid membership in a union. It goes without saying that union membership should be forbidden to personnel in the armed forces.

4. Employers should be free to make membership of a union a condition of employment (the closed shop), but equally they should be free to make non-membership a condition of employment, or to impose neither condition. The abominable evil of the closed shop as we know it arises from the tyrannical powers which unions have acquired, *de jure* or *de facto*, over both employers and workers. If this tyranny could not be removed, it would be right to forbid the closed shop absolutely, not merely to limit its ambit as under present legislation. But if the unions became true free-market service agencies for their members, and if the employers had an equal right to make union membership or non-membership a condition of employment, or to choose neither, there would be no evil in a freely agreed closed-shop arrangement. We may be sure that it would arise only where the union's service to members made them specially attractive to employers, perhaps by endowing them with a superior degree of competence or reliability. In practice it is probable that most employers would make neither membership nor non-membership of a union a condition of employment.

5. The American provision, or its like, whereby a union may have the right in law to represent non-members (whether on the ground of a majority vote or otherwise), and to require non-members to pay the equivalent of union dues (the agency shop), should not be adopted or copied in Britain. Nor should a union or its members have a right to compel an employer to administer the payment of dues by check-off. An employer should be permitted to administer a check-off only with the free agreement of each employee concerned, which should be renounceable on due notice.

6. A union or any person or persons should have the right in law, subject to contract, to call for or to instigate a concerted withdrawal of labour from any employer (except where union membership is forbidden in law), but such withdrawal should take effect as self-dismissal from the jobs concerned, unless the

employer freely agrees not to treat it as such. Similarly, an employer should have the right in law, subject to contract, to lock out any or all of his employees at will. In either case, if the withdrawal of labour or the lock-out is in breach of an agreement, the normal consequences for breach of contract by way of damages or otherwise should ensue (see Proposal 2 above). If the instigator of a withdrawal of labour thereby produces a breach of contract, he should be liable to pay damages accordingly.

7. Sympathetic withdrawals of labour and secondary boycotts should, subject to contract, be lawful. Correspondingly, employers should have the right, subject to contract, to join together in defence against any union or labour action, and to maintain and exchange worker blacklists (subject to the law of libel and slander). In present conditions of union legal privilege and widespread union violence, the sympathetic strike and the secondary boycott are intolerable invasions into the rights of others, and have properly been made unlawful. But with the strict limitations on union power suggested in this *Paper*, there would be no need to proscribe these practices.

8. Compulsory arbitration and compulsory 'cooling-off' periods should have no place in labour law. Such arrangement could, of course, be provided in free agreements.

9. The concept of unfair dismissal should have no place in labour law, unless it appears in a freely-negotiated agreement between employers and employees or their unions. Subject to contract, and in particular to due notice, employers and employees should be entitled to part from each other at will. Employers and employees and/or their unions should be free to agree upon grievance procedures governing, *inter alia*, dismissal, and providing where apposite for penalties and/or compensation.

10. All violence or the threat thereof in industrial disputes should be made a special species of criminal offence and subjected to severe penalties. Picketing should be limited to a small number of persons at the place of work of the strikers, each member of the picket to be nominated by the union (or the leadership in the case of a wildcat strike) and authorised to act as such by the police at specified places and times. Picketing by unauthorised

persons should be an offence in itself, even if peaceful. By whom-soever committed, acts of violence and attempts to prevent or hinder the free movement of persons or vehicles lawfully seeking to enter or leave the picketed premises should be subject to severe penalties. The liability of unions for picketing offences should be as follows.

(a) They should be subject to substantial fines if picketing offences are committed by their members, whether author-ised pickets or not, unless their rules require the expulsion of members who are found guilty of such offences.

(b) They should be subject to substantial fines if they promote, organise, pay for, or otherwise procure picketing by un-authorised pickets, whether composed of members or non-members.

(c) They should be subject to substantial fines, and seques-tration of assets pending acceptable assurances of good behaviour, if they counsel, promote, or organise any form of violence by pickets, whether authorised or unauthorised, and whether composed of members or non-members.

(d) Organisations other than unions which organise, promote, pay for, or otherwise procure picketing in cases of industrial disputes should be subject to substantial fines, and also sequestration of assets pending acceptable assurances of good behaviour.

(e) The available penalties should include imprisonment for officers of unions or other organisations where they counsel, promote, procure, or organise violence by their pickets.

11. Unions should have the right to set up a fund for political purposes apart from their general funds, but no member should be compelled to contribute to a political fund, and contributions thereto should be by 'contracting-in' only. Similarly, 'contracting-in' by shareholders should be required for political contributions by business companies. If this makes company contributions impracticable, so be it.

12. Social welfare payments to the families of strikers should be governed by the normal law relating to self-dismissal from em-ployment, save that, where the strike is authorised by a union,

any social welfare payments should be chargeable against and recoverable from union funds. Workers who are locked out by an employer should qualify for social welfare payments according to the normal law relating to involuntary unemployment.

13. The constitutions of unions should be subject to a body of law comparable to the law of business corporations, with a view to ensuring proper accountability for the levying of dues, expenditure of funds, use of union property, election of officers, balloting for strikes, and other matters of internal government.

14. No plans for profit-sharing, or co-partnership, or co-determination should be imposed upon employers by law, but employers, employees and employees' unions should be free to make such agreements relating thereto as they may wish.

*   *   *

Most, or perhaps all, of the above suggestions are likely even today to be described as 'politically impossible'. The cry of 'political impossibility' is the bane of good government and good social arrangements. To know what ought to be done, whether it is for the time being thought politically possible or not, is an indispensable foundation for the solution of political or social problems.

Two Commentaries on

What Right to Strike?

A LABOUR LAWYER'S COMMENT

CYRIL GRUNFELD

Professor of Law, London School of Economics, 1966-82

The purpose of Mr Shenfield's interesting reform proposals appears
to be the establishment of a free labour market by legislative means,
with the assumption that prosperity for a free, democratic society
will follow, indeed, that such prosperity can follow only from
the establishment of a free labour market. May I express some
doubts about both the feasibility of the purpose and the realism
of the assumption, while suggesting that a valid alternative
approach has been adopted?

My view is that a perfectly free labour market is not possible
in the modern state. Workers as a whole do not have perfect
labour market information available to them nor can they enjoy
perfect country-wide mobility. Furthermore, a training system,
which is only now being modernised some fifty years late, has
applied its own friction to the hopeful worker's bicycle wheels.
There is also the question of the existence of different labour
markets – for example, as between public sector and private sector
and as among small, medium and large organisations. In the real
world, as opposed to that of abstract hypothesis, prosperity must
be pursued in the absence of a perfectly free market in labour.

In contradiction to Mr Shenfield's preferred state of universal
employment 'at will', subject to contract (Proposal 9), the existence
of a law of unfair dismissal is not a significant obstacle to the
development of a prosperous economy. The need for such a law
illustrates the truism that economic problems may not always
be purely economic. There may be a political dimension that
demands a point of balance. In this instance, the political dimension takes the form of demanding acceptable standards of human
behaviour in employment. The law of unfair dismissal, introduced
by the Industrial Relations Act 1971, was an overdue reaction

[50]

to the crudity and unavoidable limitations of the common law of contract as applied to the employment relationship. But no system, including that of the law of unfair dismissal, can keep its equilibrium automatically. In applying the statutory provisions, tribunals and courts have had to balance the requirement that employers and managers behave fairly towards their subordinates against the imperative need for commercial and industrial companies as well as nationalised corporations and public bodies to be efficient if the nation is to prosper. The reintroduction of a two years' qualifying period, after a Labour Government had reduced it to an extreme six months, has also helped.

The liberation of the forces of the market and competition in all appropriate situations, whether in the public or the private sector, is of the first importance. But the market alone is too narrow an approach to law reform in instances like that of unfair dismissal, and of certain aspects of trade union organisation and industrial disruption referred to below. Also, in my view, market forces are not the rock bottom of the diagnosis of our relative economic drift downwards and, therefore, of its remedy.

Evidence world-wide has established the overriding importance of the market and of competitive forces transmitted through the market in achieving a viable level of efficiency, whether in the private or public sectors of the economy. Political suppression of the market invariably depresses the national level of prosperity well below that which would otherwise have been attained. But long experience has also suggested a level of dynamism that goes deeper than the mechanism of the market. This is, I believe, the fundamental truth, grasped more fully by the present Prime Minister than by any of her predecessors this century, that only individuals, by their flair, inventiveness, enterprise and drive, can in the ultimate analysis create sufficient wealth for an advanced nation's needs; and this applies in whatever setting an individual finds himself (or herself).

Such individuals, invariably in an indeterminate minority, have had little public power or influence in Britain as compared with politicians, civil servants and local authority officials, trade union leaders, media pundits, academic publicists and writers. The most influential and vocal elements in our society are generally not themselves wealth creators and have, until the advent of Mrs Thatcher, tended neither to sympathise with, comprehend nor support the wealth creators who, principally if not alone, can make the solid foundations for a thriving economy.

The post-1979 labour legislation is most fruitfully viewed in the context of 'Thatcherism', that is, the policy of opposing overmanned and outmoded industry, spoiling adversarial industrial relations and excessively burdensome bureaucracy, and stimulating the development of an economic and cultural environment in which the British 'Mr Hondas' can thrive and, in so doing, make a thriving nation.

The post-1979 legislation is not an anti-trade union blueprint but, broadly, a step-by-step response to the industrial and political implications of the practices of certain trade unions in the last twenty years. These practices have included mass secondary, or flying, 'pickets'; quasi-picketing 'demonstrations'; secondary (and 'tertiary') boycotting blockades; callous disruption of essential services, including obstructing hospital treatment and leaving the dead unburied; cutting the water supply and threatening to poison it with untreated sewage; 'car park' voting on industrial action; limited but non-stop disruptions in the key motor industry in particular; a vast extension of the closed shop; defiance of court orders; the wholesale violation of the union's own rulebook by the leadership in the recent mining dispute; and the occasional cruel persecution of individual union members who cross the wishes of activists.

Let us now consider in more detail Mr Shenfield's proposals in the principal areas of collective labour relations and the law.

(1) *Membership of a trade union*

The present law gives any employee, except the police, members of the armed forces and of Government Communications Headquarters (GCHQ), a strongly-guaranteed right to be a member of an independent trade union.

Vis-à-vis employers, this means that the employee will have a good complaint of unfair dismissal if dismissed for proposing to join or joining or taking part in the activities of a trade union. Reinstatement may be ordered, or compensation, which has been substantially enlarged under the Employment Act 1982.

Vis-à-vis trade unions, it means, broadly, that no employee may be excluded from membership on any 'unreasonable' ground where there is a closed shop.

[52]

As to freedom not to join a union, experience under the Industrial Relations Act 1971 of a blanket prohibition of the closed shop (subject to a few exceptions after due inquiry) demonstrated the futility of a simple 'right to work' law in Britain. The post-1979 legislation has adopted the approach of requiring a 'union membership agreement' to be approved by an 85 per cent majority of those voting (or 80 per cent of the eligible voters), subject to categories of absolute exemption concerning existing non-unionists and those who object to union membership 'on grounds of conscience or other deeply-held personal conviction'. In the wake of these provisions the closed shop has been terminated in a number of large organisations in both public and private sectors.

In large measure, then, Mr Shenfield's Proposal 3 is already embodied in current law. As to going beyond the existing degree of prohibition, this is not politically impossible, as the 1971 Act indicates, but would be a needless distraction from the overriding task of reversing Britain's economic decline. Proposal 4, it should be pointed out, is scarcely reconcilable with Proposal 3.

The closed shop is not merely an industrial relations issue. It has an equally important political dimension which displays two aspects. First, there is the liberty of the individual not to be forced against his will into an organisation with whose purposes, activities and methods he may disagree. It is an area where a fair balance must be struck between individual liberty and collective power, which is what the recent legislation has tried to do.

The second aspect refers to the dark side of trade unionism, by which I mean the use of trade union organisation to impose a régime of widespread or even total control on pain of loss of livelihood over British people, including press, radio, television and education. This is alone good reason for not allowing closed shops to be concluded or imposed without restraint, whether or not trade unions could be remoulded as 'true free market service agencies for their members'.

(2) *Recognition of a trade union*

With membership built up under legal protection, a union's next step is to secure recognition from the employer for the purpose of consultation, representation in procedure and, above all, negotiation. The Industrial Relations Act 1971 created statutory recognition machinery based on the Commission on Industrial Relations and the National Industrial Relations Court. This was abolished by the Trade Union and Labour Relations Act 1974 and replaced, under the Employment Protection Act 1975, with recognition machinery based on the Advisory, Conciliation and Arbitration Service (ACAS) and the Central Arbitration Committee, but abandoning the former restraint on union disruption conducted in parallel with the recognition procedure and excluding the employer entirely from using the machinery. Partly because of the one-sided nature of the 1975 provisions, they were repealed by the Employment Act 1980.

Recognition is now a matter for voluntary agreement between union and employer. When recognised, a union normally represents all the appropriate employees, members or non-members (*pace* Proposal 5). There are indications that certain unions might wish to exclude non-members from the fruits of their negotiations but, under present law, the employer might be exposed to a complaint before a tribunal of compelling an *unwilling* employee to join the recognised union by 'action short of dismissal'.

(3) *Collective agreements*

Proposal 2, that collective agreements should be legally binding contracts 'fully enforceable against employers, unions and individual union members', pays, with respect, insufficient attention to existing law and the feasibility of the proposal. Suing an individual employee for the loss caused by disruption in breach of a collective agreement is unreal.

Again, the substantive provisions of collective agreements about terms and conditions of employment are already enforceable as between employer and employee but only at the level of the individual contract of employment into which such collectively agreed terms normally become incorporated, expressly or impliedly; and the same is probably the case for those *procedural* provisions that concern the individual employee as such, like disciplinary procedures.

A difficult question arises in respect of procedural provisions relating to collective disputes, notably, the 'peace obligation', i.e. the no-industrial-action-until-procedure-exhausted type of provision. Such a clause is 'binding in honour alone' at present.

[54]

It might be salutary for employers (including the Crown) and trade unions to have to abide by their procedures for settling disputes on pain of legal redress. However, agreed procedures are generally observed and the final effect of Proposal 2 might easily be to lead to the excision of all such clauses from collective agreements. It is difficult to perceive in the proposal any worthwhile gain in improvement of performance in Britain.

The agreements which the electricians' trade union (the EETPTU) has pioneered, and which the engineering union (the AUEW) is beginning to follow, is a different matter and most promising. The provisions about Joint Advisory Committees, single-status labour force and 'pendulum' arbitration constitute a British form of co-determination (not the crude 'no-strike' agreement vilified by the EETPTU's opponents in the TUC). It is fortunate for the country that the union which could switch off our energy supply overnight has fallen into such responsible and thoughtful hands. Mr Shenfield gravely under-estimates the union's achievements to date. The 'co-determination' agreements, the professional attention paid to the highest standards of training (and re-training) in the union's own training college, the agreement with employers in the electrical contracting industry to substitute systematic training and certified competence and qualifications for the obsolete traditional apprenticeship, all mark out the EETPTU as the outstanding British trade union since the Second World War. If all TUC unions were to follow the EETPTU approach, and that developing in the AUEW, this would be the single most beneficial and heartening change for the better in British industrial relations.

(4) *Strike, lockout and other industrial action*

Proposal 6 fails to address itself to a fundamental constitutional principle. The principle is that the industrial power enjoyed by trade unions is not to be used directly for purely or predominantly political ends.

Ours is a Parliamentary democracy. Political issues must be exposed, debated, decided and legislated upon in the open political arena of Parliament and those involved at this centre of the political process must be accountable to the electorate. If trade union leaders are free to use their union's industrial muscle directly for political ends, it is the beginning of the disenfranchisement of the people, including trade union members. This is why collective labour law confers freedom to strike or boycott only when it is in contemplation or furtherance of a 'trade dispute' whose definition is careful to omit political purposes and political disputes.

Proposal 6 fails also to consider the paramountcy of the wishes of trade union members called on to take part in a strike or other industrial action. The Trade Union Act 1984 gives union members the right to a secret ballot and employers a remedy against the union if their firm or organisation is disrupted without such a ballot in favour. The value of this provision has been adequately demonstrated. A proposal about strikes which ignores the workers themselves is seriously defective.

Proposal 6 also fails to make clear whether a lawful strike or lockout might be instantaneous or whether notice and, if so, what notice would be needed. The question of a special strike or lockout notice might be for consideration.

Financing strikes out of public funds

Proposal 12 would continue the, by world standards, special silliness of British law in giving substantial support from public money to those who withdraw their labour voluntarily for personal gain. For example, the recent needless and lawless mining dispute, estimated to have cost the nation about £6 billion, was assisted from the nation's funds to the tune of some £50-60 million in forms like supplementary benefit and mortgage interest payments, and this even after deducting £15-16 a week from each striker's supplementary benefit under the 'deeming' rule in the Social Security (No. 2) Act 1980. Mr Shenfield's proviso in Proposal 12 that social welfare payments should be recoverable from union funds lacks credibility. Even the union funds salted away in foreign bank accounts by the NUM leaders at the outset of their dispute amounted to less than £9 million.

(5) Boycotts and blockades

I take leave to doubt the wisdom of Proposal 7. It cannot be sensible to tolerate any amount of boycotting and blockading when there is an industrial dispute. Industrial conflict does not take place in a vacuum. There is a natural public interest in establishing limits to society's destabilisation when managers and union leaders and their members disagree.

In the Employment Act 1980, instead of simply outlawing secondary boycotts and blockades as other countries have done, a balance was struck between recognising British union solidarity up to the first supplier or customer of an employer in dispute but making more extensive boycotting unlawful, essentially, in the national interest. It is, again, part of the political dimension of industrial relations in relation to which Mr Shenfield's 'strict limitations on union power' seem irrelevant.

It may be added that the new law about pre-industrial action ballots, secondary boycotts and picketing would not have been effective if trade unions as such had not been made legally responsible in tort for the unlawful acts of their agents by the Employment Act 1982. This has been the pivotal provision. Proposal 1 recognises this but is otherwise perplexing (as is also Proposal 2 since trade unions have been liable in contract since the 19th century).

(6) *Picketing*

There are two parts to the law governing the conduct of picketing, a civil law part and a criminal law part.

As to the civil law part, the Employment Act 1980 has replaced the thoughtlessly permissive provision originating in the Trade Disputes Act 1906 with the basic rule that workers may only picket their own place of work along with their union representatives and may only do so in a reasonable way. If they violate this rule, or if union members picket someone else's workplace, the employer concerned may seek his remedy in tort against the union. The suggestion in Proposal 10, that picketing might be made criminal *per se*, is, with respect, misconceived.

As to the criminal law part, this is the general criminal law relevant to keeping the Queen's Peace on the public highway or, in more modern terminology, the law governing public order, like the offences of obstructing the highway, conduct likely to cause a breach of the peace, obstructing a police constable in the execution of his duty, offences against the person and against property up to unlawful assembly, affray or riot. If union officials organise or promote such criminal conduct, they will themselves be guilty of the offences or of criminal conspiracy. The problem is usually one of evidence. Proposal 10 is largely superfluous.

(7) *Proposals 11, 13 and 14*

Proposal 11 about 'contracting-in' for both trade union members and company shareholders is well taken.

Proposals 13 and 14 refer to important subjects that demand far more thorough analysis and detailed consideration, as Mr Shenfield would doubtless agree. Thus, an analysis of trade union government and administration would quickly reveal the need to take account of the new rulebook introduced last year by the leaders of the NUM. It is probably the most autocratic and potentially oppressive constitutional instrument in the history of British trade unions, which, unless legally checked, will set a sinister precedent for any autocratically minded union leaders.

Again, the question of how to inform, involve and motivate employees is absolutely vital if Britain is to succeed in climbing back up the economic league table. Mr Shenfield's caveat that a planner's blueprint is inappropriate is well taken. It would need a separate paper to do justice to this theme, including the pernicious proposals of the Bullock Committee. An exceptional union leader may always be invited on to a company's board as a non-executive director. But most union leaders and officials have at present little 'feel' for business and would be likely to become a dead hand on a company if given statutory places on the boards of big companies. Involvement of employees with their relevant expertise and stake in their organisation's success is an entirely different matter.

Conclusion

We have reached a critical watershed in our economic history. Decades of relative decline have gradually caught up with us. By 1979 it appeared that the 'skids' were under our country. Mrs Thatcher has for the time being stemmed what had become the hopelessness of our position through pursuing erroneous policies for so long. Mr Shenfield's proposals are clearly intended to try to hold us on our new and hopeful course. But the substance of those proposals appear to me not to help at all in their over-narrow free-market approach and detachment from the existing relevant legal provisions.

March 1986   CYRIL GRUNFELD

THINKING ABOUT THE UNTHINKABLE

SIR LEONARD NEAL

This *Paper* should be judged against the background of the last 25 years during which the trade unions and their apologists have achieved extraordinary success in persuading governments, the media, the Church – and the public generally – of the correctness in elevating the right to strike into a 'public good'. From this standpoint, Mr Shenfield's paper is not merely timely and conclusively argued, but something that should be compulsory reading in Whitehall, in Fleet Street, in the BBC, and in the Synod of the Church of England.

During this lamentable quarter of a century we have seen leading British industries ruined, governments humiliated and brought down, the police and the public attacked, and the so-called 'right to strike' made superior to all other rights, including the right to work and, indeed, the right to live (witness the claim by a trade union official in the North West during a local authority and hospital strike that, 'if some people die as a consequence of our strike that may be the price the public will have to pay for our strike to succeed').

In pursuit of this extraordinary philosophy, governments and parliaments from 1947 to 1979 did not hesitate to impose on work-people, managements and the economy generally the most onerous burdens. They have ranged from different varieties of incomes policies, ministerial intervention to constrain the police and the public from defending people's rights, to coercive laws on companies and individuals in order to support the notion that trade unionism is an absolute good and striking an absolute right. Thus we can imagine the outcry that Mr Shenfield's polemic will provoke, almost as a latter-day Martin Luther who dares to question the received wisdom that has been thrust down our throats in these years. Moreover, it was a 'wisdom' that ensnared most of us. In some mysterious way we have been too ready to accept these trade union arguments as though they were God-given and not to be questioned.

The list of rights and powers demanded and often granted is endless: 'Trade Unions are now an Estate of the Realm'; trade unions cannot be required to conform to the laws that constrain the rest of us; 'they must be completely free to pursue their policies and their aims'; 'they need immunities'; the rights of individuals may not be equated with the rights of trade unions; the trade unions must be free to challenge and obstruct the plans of companies before those plans are implemented; they must have rights of co-determination. But none of these 'rights' has so beguiled the public mind as the so-called fundamental right to withdraw labour – that is, the 'right to strike'.

Fortunately, this theology is now questioned by Mr Shenfield. That his argument must be correct needs only to be tested by extending the claim to an unfettered right to strike to its ultimate horror, that of a simultaneous strike of power workers, hospital workers, firemen, water workers, *et al*. Such a consideration is by no means bizarre, if we remember that, until a few years ago, strikes in some of those services were unknown and unthinkable. Since then most of these workers have enjoyed the 'benefits' of striking and only the fortuitous presence of a moderate leadership in power generation and supply has ensured that we have not been blacked out. But it needs to be remembered that trade union leaders are transient beings and that the capacity of trade unions to swing entirely from right to left and back again in harmony with the prejudices of newly elected/appointed leaders is a characteristic of British trade unions.

And so, again, Mr Shenfield performs a great service by thinking about the unthinkable and by drawing attention to, amongst other things, the urgency of seeking a limitation of these 'rights' of trade unions in certain public services. But here I find it necessary to separate membership of a trade union from the right to strike, for these two rights – membership and striking – are not concomitants of each other. It seems perfectly feasible that membership could exist together with rights of representation, but without the right to strike in some sensitive services, where interruption of work because of a withdrawal of labour could seriously threaten public safety and individual lives.

[61]

Finally, industrial terrorism, like political terrorism, will not go away of its own accord. We must therefore be vigorous as well as vigilant in protesting public and individual rights that really are fundamental compared to the extravagant and bogus right to strike of trade unions.

Many ordinary British people will join me in hoping that Mr Shenfield's critique will be followed by an equally forthright and equally effective demolition of two other evils that afflict us, those of so-called 'racial equality' and 'equal opportunities'.

TOPICS FOR DISCUSSION

1. It is alleged that existing unions tend to be undemocratic bodies, unless the law forces some democracy upon them. Discuss
   (a) the truth or untruth of this allegation, and
   (b) its relevance, if any, to the nature of the strike weapon.

2. Discuss the validity, if any, of strikers' claims to a property in their jobs.

3. Picketing is lawful only if it is peaceful. Do you believe that this requirement of the law can be enforced in practice? If so, what measures would you recommend for this purpose?

4. It is alleged that all legislative attempts at employment 'protection' amount to employment destruction. Analyse this hypothesis.

5. Is it true that the individual worker has a natural or normal bargaining disadvantage *vis-à-vis* the employer?

6. Debate the case for and against the right of an employer to impose
   (a) membership or
   (b) non-membership of a union as a condition of employment.

7. Debate the case for and against legal immunities as a governing principle for the rights of unions.

8. Evaluate the legal concept of 'unfair dismissal' and examine its legal consequences.

9. Do trade unions raise productivity?

10. Should the law of tort apply to unions and their members equally with all other bodies and persons? Argue the case for and against this proposition.

FURTHER READING

Other IEA publications which analyse the law and economics of trade union organisation include:

Hutt, W. H., *The Theory of Collective Bargaining 1930-1975*, Hobart Paperback 8, 1975.

Robbins, Lord, *et al.*, *Trade Unions: Public Goods or Public 'Bads'?*, IEA Readings 17, 1978.

Hayek, F. A., *1980s Unemployment and the Unions*, Hobart Paper 87, 1980 (second edition, 1984).

The debate on trade unions, society and the economy is reviewed in

Addison, J. T., and Burton, J., *Trade Unions and Society: Some Lessons of the British Experience*, The Fraser Institute, Vancouver, B.C., Canada, 1984,

and analysed definitively in

Addison, J. T., and Hirsch, B., *The Economic Analysis of Unions: New Approaches and Evidence*, Allen and Unwin, London, 1986.

Other economic and legal analyses of various aspects of the subject include:

Hutt, W. H., *The Strike Threat System*, Arlington House, New Rochelle, New York, 1974.

Reynolds, Morgan O., *Power and Privilege*, Universe Books, New York, 1984.

Rosa, Jean-Jacques (ed.), *The Economics of Trade Unions: New Directions*, Kluwer-Nijhoff Publishing, Boston, The Hague, Dordrecht, Lancaster, 1984.

Mulvey, Charles, *The Economic Analysis of Trade Unions*, Martin Robertson, Oxford, 1978.

Rees, Albert, *The Economics of Trade Unions*, University of Chicago Press, Chicago, Illinois, 1962.

Bradley, P. D. (ed.), *The Public Stake in Union Power*, University of Virginia Press, Charlottesville, Virginia, 1959.

Grunfeld, Cyril, *Modern Trade Union Law*, Sweet and Maxwell, London, 1966.

Drake, Charles D., *The Trade Union Acts*, Sweet and Maxwell, London, 1985.